MICROHABITATS

Life in a
SAND DUNE

Malcolm Penny

Raintree
Chicago, Illinois

© 2004 Raintree
Published by Raintree, a division of Reed Elsevier, Inc.
Chicago, Illinois
Customer Service 888-363-4266
Visit our website at www.raintreelibrary.com

All rights reserved. No part of this publication may be reproduced or utilized in any form or by any means, electronic or mechanical, including photocopying, recording, or by any information storage and retrieval system, without permission in writing from the publishers.

For information, address the publisher:
Raintree, 100 N. LaSalle, Suite 1200, Chicago, IL 60602

Project Editors: Geoff Barker, Marta Segal Block, Jennifer Mattson, Kathryn Walker
Production Manager: Brian Suderski
Illustrated by Dick Twinney
Consultant: Michael Chinery
Designed by Ian Winton
Picture research by Rachel Tisdale

Planned and produced by Discovery Books

Library of Congress Cataloging-in-Publication Data:
Penny, Malcolm.
Life in a sand dune / Malcolm Penny.
v. cm. -- (Microhabitats)
Includes bibliographical references.
Contents: The sand dune -- Plant life -- Invertebrate life -- Larger residents -- Visitors to the dunes -- Dunes under threat.
ISBN 0-7398-6805-5 (lib. bdg.) -- ISBN 1-4109-0350-8 (pbk.)
1. Sand dune ecology--Juvenile literature. [1. Sand dune ecology. 2. Ecology.] I. Title. II. Series.
QH541.5.S26P46 2004
577.5'83--dc21
2003003640

Printed and bound in the United States.

08 07 06 05 04
10 9 8 7 6 5 4 3 2 1

Acknowledgments
The publishers would like to thank the following for permission to reproduce their pictures:
Front cover: Nigel J.Dennis/Natural History Photographic Agency; p.6: Alberto Nardi/Natural History Photographic Agency; p.8: Anthony Bannister/Natural History Photographic Agency; p.9: Martin Harvey/Natural History Photographic Agency; p.10: Judith Clark/Bruce Coleman Collection; p.11: Karl Switak/Natural History Photographic Agency; p.12: Kim Taylor/Bruce Coleman Collection; p.13: Oxford Scientific Films; p.14: M.Moffett/Frank Lane Picture Agency; p.16: Nigel J.Dennis/Natural History Photographic Agency; p.17: Mark Newman/Frank Lane Picture Agency; p.18: Joe McDonald/Bruce Coleman Collection; p.19: Raymond Mendez AA/Oxford Scientific Films; p.20: Carol Hughes/Bruce Coleman Collection; p.21: Daniel Heuclin/Natural History Photographic Agency; p.22: Claude Steelman SAL/Oxford Scientific Films; p.24: Jurgen and Christine Sohns/Frank Lane Picture Agency; p.25: Chris Mattison/Frank Lane Picture Agency; p.26: David Hosking/Frank Lane Picture Agency; p.27: Mark Newman/Frank Lane Picture Agency; p.28: Anthony Bannister/Natural History Photographic Agency; p.29: Fritz Polking/Frank Lane Picture Agency.

Some words are shown in bold, **like this.** You can find out what they mean by looking in the glossary

Contents

The Sand Dune	4
Plant Life	10
Invertebrate Life	12
Larger Dune Dwellers	18
Dune Visitors	24
Dunes Under Threat	26
Glossary	30
Further Reading	31
Index	32

The Sand Dune

Where Sand Meets Wind

Wherever sand and wind meet, dunes grow. The landscape they build is never still. It shifts slowly every day. Its changing patterns are governed by the direction and strength of the wind, and by how coarse or fine the sand is. Some sand dunes develop by the ocean or on the shores of lakes, and others develop far inland.

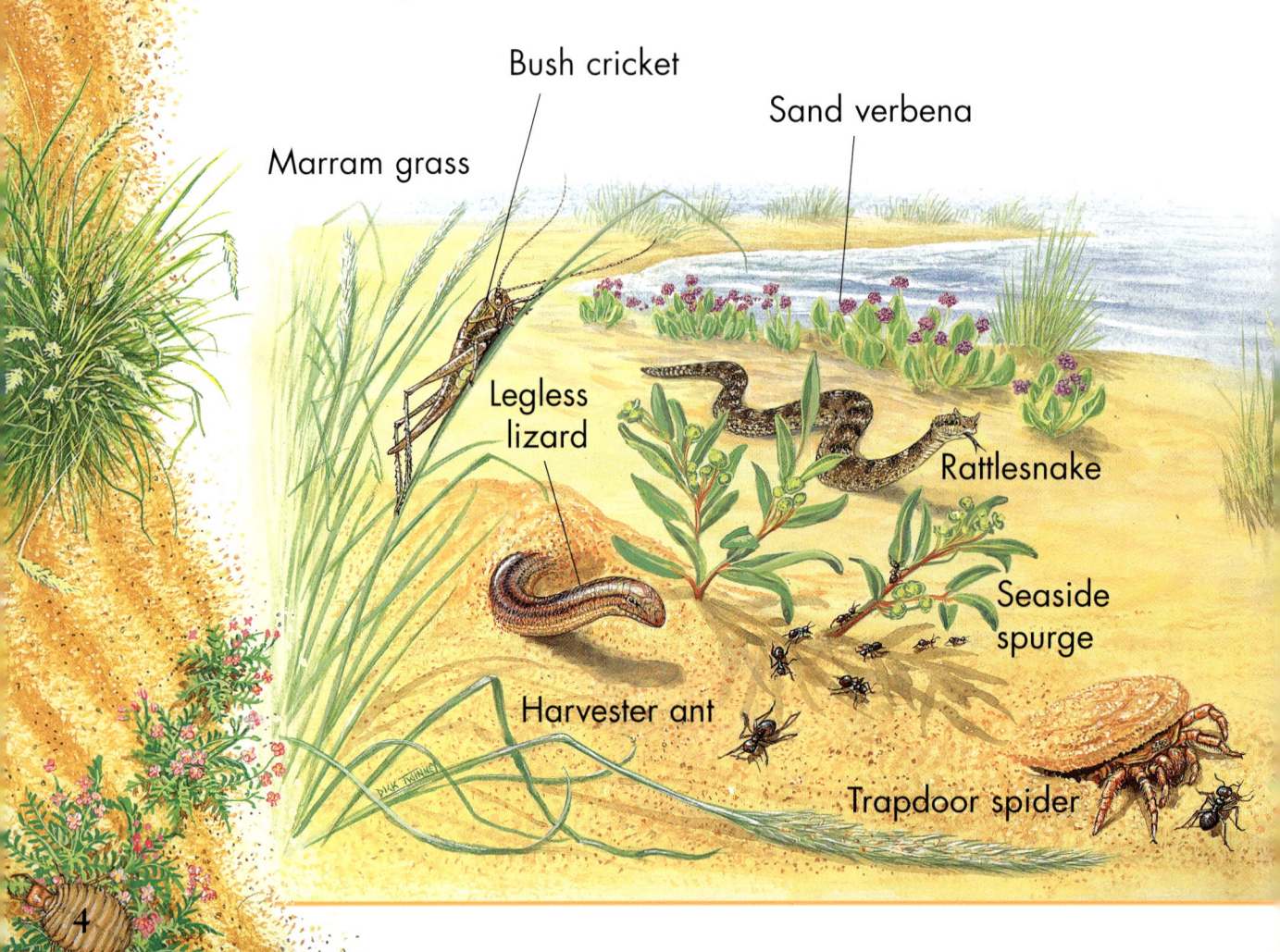

- Bush cricket
- Sand verbena
- Marram grass
- Legless lizard
- Rattlesnake
- Seaside spurge
- Harvester ant
- Trapdoor spider

A Hostile Home

A sand dune is a difficult place to live. Water is scarce, and food hard to find. It is a place for **specialists**—animals and plants that have their own ways of solving the problems of living in this dry, shifting environment. Sand dunes are home to an amazing variety of plants and animals that have **adapted** to survive in what at first sight seems to be a very hostile **microhabitat.**

Guess What?

The highest sand dunes in North America reach to 800 ft (250 m), in Great Sand Dunes National Monument, Colorado.

The largest expanse of sand dunes in North America is Gran Desierto in Mexico, part of the Sonoran Desert.

The fastest moving sand dunes travel at 300 ft (30 m) per year, but many do not move at all.

Kangaroo rat

Sand wasp

Tiger beetle

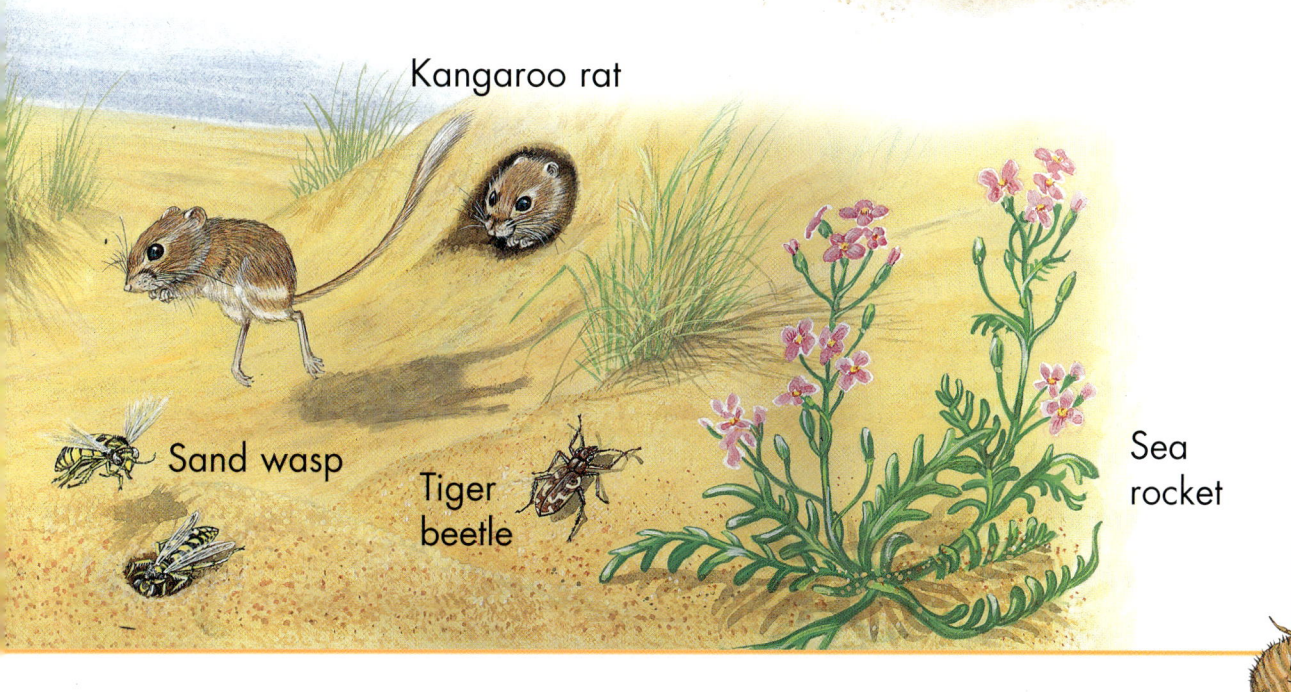

Sea rocket

A Dune is Born

Fragments of rock **eroded,** or worn away, from mountains and hillsides are washed down rivers and into the ocean, to join other particles that the ocean has worn from cliffs. The movement of the water rubs them together and polishes them into round sand grains. Sand thrown onto the shore by storms and high tides dries out above the high water mark. Then the wind picks it up and carries it inland.

Not all sand dunes are by the ocean. Some are in deserts far from any water, perhaps in places that were once oceans long ago, or where sand has gathered after traveling on the wind miles from the shore.

A clump of grass traps blowing sand so that a small mound builds up around it and a new dune begins to form.

Dune-building

If sand grains land on a hard surface, they bounce and move on. On a soft surface, they stop. Dry sand is a soft surface, so in any small hollow in the ground, or around any obstacle where some sand has gathered, more will stop. The dune has begun to grow. Grains from the side of the dune facing into the wind, or **windward** side, blow over the top and tumble down the opposite, or **downwind,** side, to form what is known as the **slip face.**

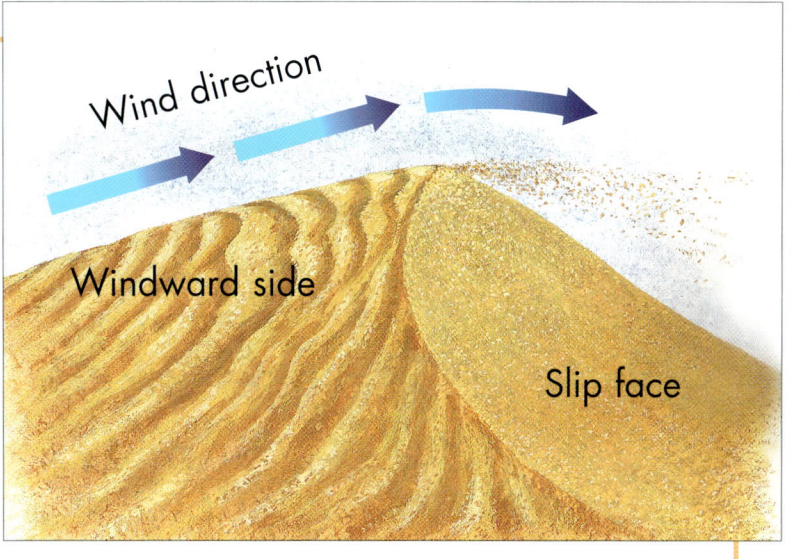

See for Yourself

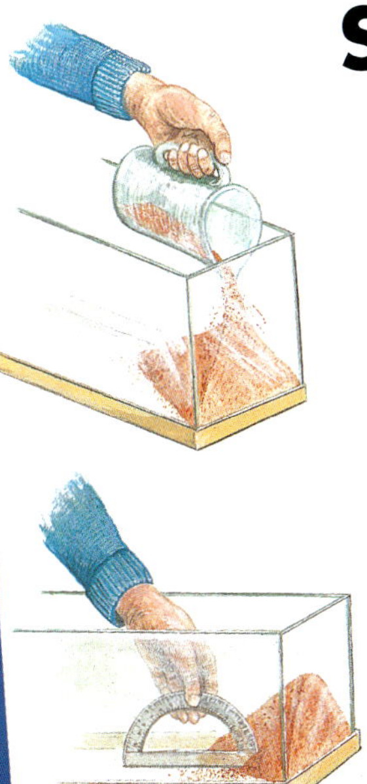

To see how sand settles, get an empty glass aquarium. Carefully add some sand into one end of the aquarium and watch the sand form a sloping pile. Measure the angle of the slope with a protractor. If the sand is dry, the slope is never more than 32°. Slightly damp sand will form a steeper slope, but when it is really wet, it starts to slide down until it becomes level.

Living in Shifting Sands

The surface of a sand dune is constantly exposed to sun and wind, except on the **slip face.** This is where all the animals live, out of the wind but often in a rain of falling sand grains. They are active only in the morning and evening, when the sun is not too high. The dune animals spend the hottest parts of the day underground, where the sand is cooler.

The gerbil spends its days away from the heat of the desert in its burrow. It emerges in the cool evening to gather food.

Some lizards that live on dunes move through the loose sand as if they were swimming. If disturbed, they dive head first into the sand and disappear. Other dune animals dig **burrows** to hide in during the day, though this is not easy in loose, tumbling sand.

Food from the Air

The wind that built the dune is the daily enemy of the animals that live there, but in one way it is also their friend. The sand grains that tumble down the slip face are not all that the wind carries. It also transports seeds and bits of dead plants which are vital food for many dune animals.

Guess What?

Although sand dunes in some regions are regularly rained or even snowed on, all the animals that live in them must be able to survive a water shortage, because sand dries out again so quickly.

Some windblown dunes make humming or moaning sounds caused by the constant movement of sand particles. These are sometimes called "singing dunes."

Sand-diving lizards often cool down by lifting two feet at a time off the hot sand.

Plant Life

Pioneer Plants

The first plants to grow on a new dune are known as "**pioneer** plants." The most important is marram grass, sometimes called American beach grass. It is so good for stabilizing or holding the sand in place that some call it "the dune builder." Marram grass only grows near oceans, but similar types of pioneer plants grow on desert dunes away from the sea.

Marram grass helps stabilize dunes all over the world. The plant also changes the temperature and moisture of the dunes where it grows.

Changing Conditions

The roots of dune grasses trap rainwater, stopping it from sinking through the sand, and their leaves slowly release **water vapor** into the air. This added water vapor makes the dune surface firmer and cooler, and much more welcoming to other plants and animals—though they still need to be **specialists** to survive.

Among these specialists are plants like seaside spurge, which grows flat against the ground to keep out of the wind; sea rocket, which can store water in its thick, waxy leaves; and tumbleweed, which has very narrow leaves to avoid being dried out by the sun.

Guess What?

In the Namib Desert, a plant called the nara bush sends its roots deep underground until it can reach water. It produces fruit that look like small striped melons, and are full of sweet juice. Nara fruits are a valuable source of water for all kinds of desert animals, including tiny mice, jackals, and even elephants.

The flowers of sand verbena form a purple carpet in Palm Springs, California.

Invertebrate Life

Burrowing Wasps

Sand wasps, often called digger wasps, **burrow** into the sand, supporting the sides of the burrow with wax to keep it from caving in. The wasp makes this wax inside its own body, scrapes it from an area on its **abdomen,** and molds it with its jaws.

Sand wasps are hunters, going out in the evening in search of caterpillars or spiders. When a female catches a caterpillar, she **paralyzes** it with a sting, and carries or drags it back to her burrow. There she buries it, with one of her eggs. When the egg hatches, the wasp **larva** feeds on the caterpillar.

A digger wasp has dug a burrow by kicking out sand with her legs. Now she will hunt a caterpillar for her larva to feed on when it hatches.

Trapdoor Spiders

Some spiders also live in burrows, which they dig with their large fangs. The trapdoor spider spins silk to line its burrow and closes the entrance with a hinged trapdoor made of silk and sand. The spider waits inside for an insect or small lizard to pass by. Then it flips back the trapdoor, pounces on its **prey,** and drags it inside to eat.

A trapdoor spider prepares to shut the lid of its burrow and wait for its prey.

To our eyes a spider's closed trapdoor would blend into the sand all around, but some wasps can find them. They flip them open, and grab the spider as prey.

Guess What?

One kind of trapdoor spider — often called the cartwheel spider — living in the dunes of Namibia in Africa, escapes from danger by pulling in its legs and rolling down the slip face of the dune to safety.

Some trapdoor spiders dig burrows more than 8 in (20 cm) deep, and can live for several years.

Beetles

Beetles are well **adapted** to living in sand dunes. Some feed on bits of dead plants and animals blown there by the wind while others are hunters, but all need to escape the heat. They can easily **burrow** into the sand, because their hard wing cases protect them against the scratchy grains.

A long-legged darkling beetle in the Namib Desert, in southwest Africa, waits patiently to drink in the early morning dew.

Mist Drinkers

Some beetles get all the water they need from the seeds or insects that they eat, but some darkling beetles use another method. They live on dunes by the sea where mist sweeps in from the ocean during the night. In the morning mist they stand with their heads down and **abdomens** in the air. As the mist **condenses** (turns into liquid) on their bodies, it trickles down grooves in their wing cases to their mouths.

Beware of Tigers

An adult tiger beetle is an active **predator.** It has large jaws, very good eyesight, and it can run very fast. The **larva** lives quite differently. It hatches in a burrow in the sand, and waits with its jaws level with the surface. When an insect walks by, it drags it into the burrow.

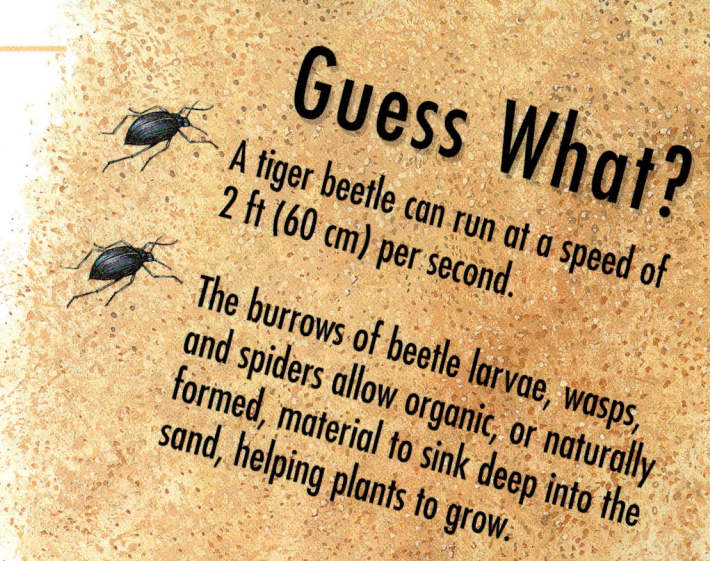

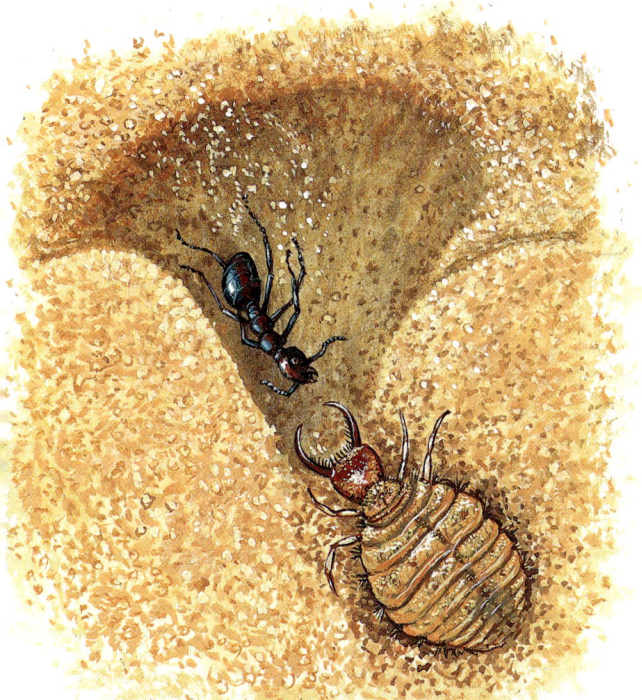

Guess What?

A tiger beetle can run at a speed of 2 ft (60 cm) per second.

The burrows of beetle larvae, wasps, and spiders allow organic, or naturally formed, material to sink deep into the sand, helping plants to grow.

Booby Trap

An adult ant lion looks like a dragonfly, but the larva lies in a pit in dry sand shaped like a cone. When an ant walks into the trap, it cannot climb out again, because the sand grains roll under its feet like marbles. Eventually the ant slides down into the waiting jaws of the ant lion larva.

An ant becomes an easy meal for the ant lion larva waiting at the bottom of its sandy pit.

Other Dune Insects

Crickets and grasshoppers are another large group of well-**adapted** dune animals, found on grassy dunes. Dune plants are usually tough to eat, and they grow in scattered clumps. Grasshoppers and crickets have two things in their favor: they have strong jaws for crunching up these tough plants, and they are often able to travel long distances in search of food.

Ants are very common all over the world, including dune areas. They also live in **burrows,** and like spiders and wasps, they must be able to keep their burrows from filling up with loose sand. Instead of using silk or wax to strengthen the burrow walls, they dig in old river or pond beds where the ground is firmer.

Grasshoppers need to be warmed by the air around them before they can make the energy they need to fly. In hot climates they can fly long distances.

Laying a Trail

In other environments, ants searching for food follow trails marked days or maybe weeks before with the scent of their nestmates. In the shifting sands of dunes though, they have to lay a fresh trail for every journey if they are to stay together. The leader of a group of workers makes one by dragging her **abdomen** along the ground.

Ants have dug out their nests in the bed of a dried-up pool in Arizona. They will have to move on when it rains.

Ant Farmers

Some ants hunt the dunes for bits of dead plants and animals or living **prey**. Others visit particular plants daily to tend groups of plant bugs (aphids) which produce a sweet liquid called honeydew that the ants collect and drink. Collecting the honeydew in this way is sometimes called "milking," because the ants seem to behave like human dairy farmers.

Guess What?

In cooler climates, grasshoppers can get warm enough to fly only on a few hot days in summer, but in hot climates they can regularly fly long distances.

The most numerous grasshopper in the world is the desert locust, which flies long distances in huge swarms from one grassy area to another. It is a serious threat to grain crops all over Africa.

Larger Dune Dwellers

Lizards

Lizards are well suited to life in shifting sand because they are covered in smooth, shiny scales. They can slide through the sand grains without being scratched by them, as if they were swimming.

Lizards cannot make their own body heat. They need to lie in the morning sun, or **bask,** before their muscles can work properly. Some lizards can darken the color of their skin, which helps them to absorb more heat. Later in the day, when they need to hide from the intense heat of the sun, they can **burrow** down into the sand where it is cooler.

A Texas horned lizard soaks up the rays of the morning sun.

Poisonous Tears

A highly specialized lizard that lives in sand dunes and deserts in North America is the horned lizard, which feeds on ants. Because ants are tiny and not very nourishing, the lizard needs to eat more than 200 ants every day—so it must be able to stay for long periods in full view of **predators,** without being harmed. If attacked, a horned lizard can squirt blood from its eyes to frighten its attacker into dropping it immediately.

The red droplets in this picture are blood which the horned lizard has squirted from its eyes to alarm its attacker.

See for Yourself

Lizards that can change their color turn darker when they are basking in the sun. If you lay out one dark-colored object and one light-colored object in the sun you will understand why. Try using different-colored shoes. After an hour or two touch them to find out which one feels the warmest. That will be the one that has absorbed the most heat.

Snakes

Snakes, like lizards, have smooth, shiny scales to protect them from the gritty sand, so they are able to live in dune environments. Some, like the **venomous** fer de lance, **burrow** in the sand, and invade other animals' burrows in search of **prey.** Others hunt out in the open.

Most snakes wriggle along in a series of S-bends, or glide forward in a straight line, but the sidewinder rattlesnake moves differently when it is in a hurry. It raises its body in loops and swings them forward one at a time, using the two body loops as legs, as if it were walking, This is quicker than wriggling.

Sidewinding leaves an unmistakable track in the desert sand.

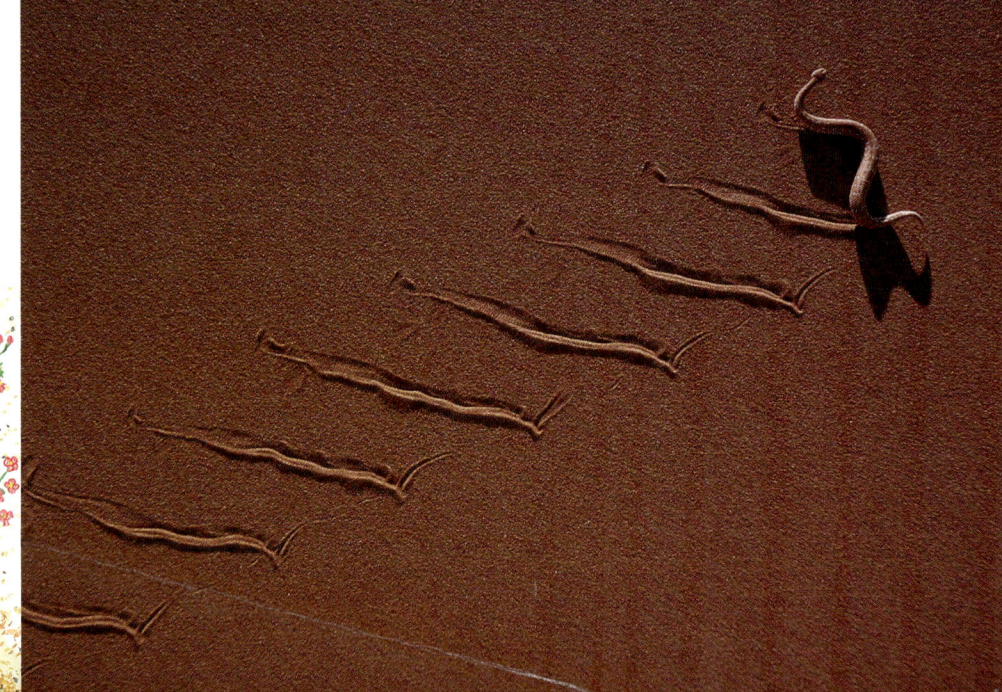

Hunting Equipment

Many people think that all snakes are venomous, but only a few of them really are. Rattlesnakes, including sidewinders, are venomous snakes.

Rattlesnakes use a few different methods to find prey. They have two pits just below their eyes containing organs that are sensitive to heat, helping them locate animals by the warmth of their bodies. Like all snakes, they also use their tongues to "smell" the air, flicking them in and out of their mouths to pick up the scent of any nearby prey.

Guess What?

People think that sidewinders move very fast, but really they usually only move at 2 miles per hour (3 kilometers per hour.)

The fastest land snake is the African black mamba, which can reach 10 miles per hour (16 kilometers per hour.)

An American sidewinder shows the heat-sensitive pits below its eyes.

Resourceful Rodent

Not many mammals can live comfortably in sand dunes, because water is hard to find, but rodents are able to do so. This is mainly because over many generations their bodies have gradually developed, or **evolved,** ways of managing with little or no water. One such creature is the kangaroo rat.

Kangaroo rats got their name because they have very long hind legs that they use to hop like little kangaroos. They get the moisture they need from their food, mainly seeds and fallen fruits, and sometimes insects. They stuff the seeds that they find into pouches in their cheeks to take back to the nest, where they eat some and store the rest.

A kangaroo rat can travel quickly over the dune in search of seeds to eat and to store for later.

In a burrow lined with soft, dry grass, a mother kangaroo rat cares for her young.

Plentiful Prey

Kangaroo rats, and other rodents, are the main food of rattlesnakes and birds of **prey.** Like other prey animals, they breed very quickly because they are not likely to live very long. Even those that escape being eaten by a **predator** will live for only a few months. They live in **burrows** underground, each pair producing as many as three **litters** of two to four young in a year.

Guess What?

A small kind of kangaroo rat, the pygmy kangaroo rat, sometimes called a kangaroo mouse, is only 3 in (7 cm) long.

The temperature inside a kangaroo rat burrow stays at 86°F (30°C) day and night, even in the summer.

Dune Visitors

Birds of Prey

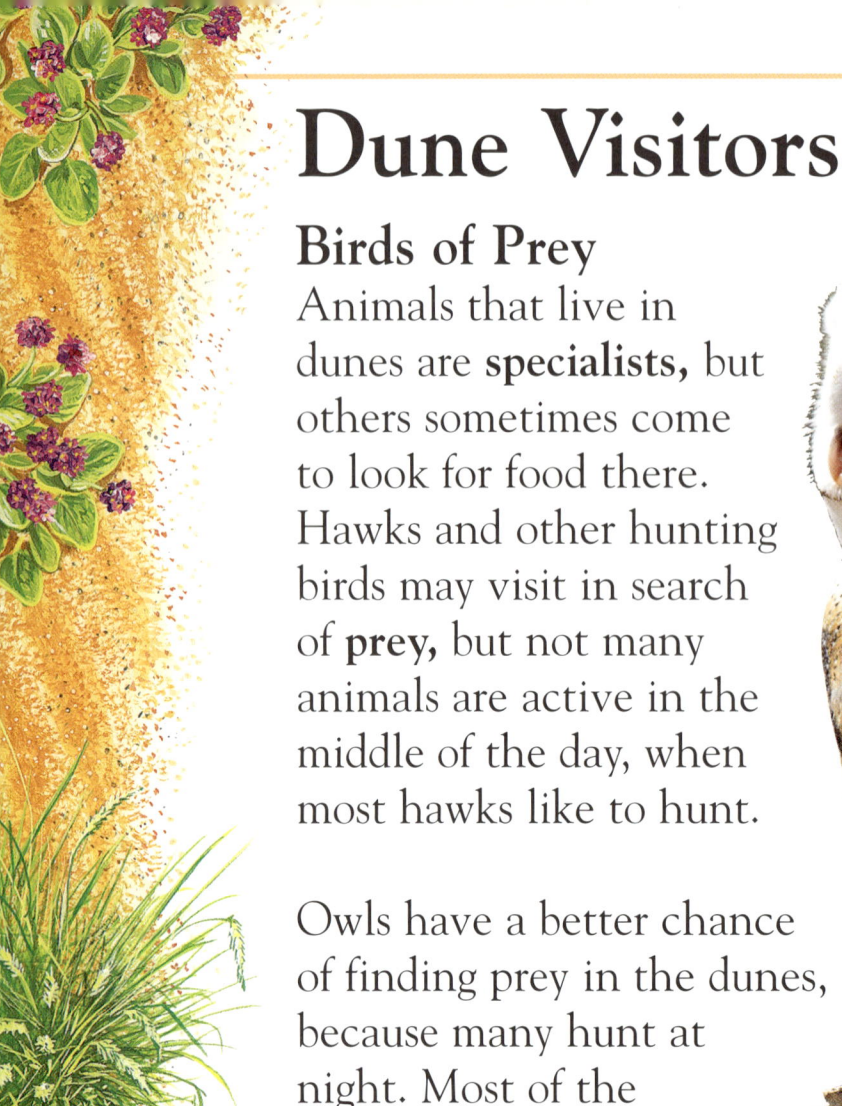

Animals that live in dunes are **specialists,** but others sometimes come to look for food there. Hawks and other hunting birds may visit in search of **prey,** but not many animals are active in the middle of the day, when most hawks like to hunt.

Owls have a better chance of finding prey in the dunes, because many hunt at night. Most of the animals stay under cover if they can, but kangaroo rats often **forage,** or look for food, in the open. However, they have very sensitive hearing. Although owls fly very quietly, the rats can often hear them coming and make their escape.

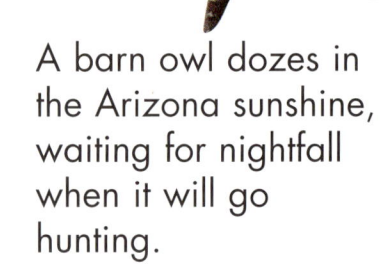

A barn owl dozes in the Arizona sunshine, waiting for nightfall when it will go hunting.

Toads by the Sea

Amphibians need fresh or only slightly salty water to breed, so you would not expect to find them in dunes. In Europe, however, natterjack toads are an exception. They live for most of the year in sandy **burrows,** and in the spring they gather to breed in the small, temporary pools that form in coastal dunes.

Guess What?

The enormous dunes in Namibia, in southwest Africa, attract some unexpected visitors. Hunting lions are often seen there, and elephants tramp across the dunes from one waterhole to another.

Natterjack toads sing in a chorus at sunset. Their calls can be heard from more than 1 mi (1.5 km) away on a quiet evening.

The natterjack toad breeds in the warm, shallow ponds that form in sand dunes.

Human Visitors

Although dunes are not welcoming places for those that need to find food, shelter, and somewhere to breed, they are very beautiful and exciting. Because of this, they attract many human visitors. This is not always a good thing.

Dunes Under Threat

Upsetting the Balance

Sand dunes are sometimes seen as a threat to people, because they can invade farmland or block roads when they are blown by the wind. This can happen naturally, but it happens more quickly when people remove the plants that hold the dunes in place. The first settlers on the Oregon coast did this, and by the 1930s the dunes there were moving around and causing problems. People planted beach grass and other kinds of plants to keep the sand stable.

Kolmanskop in Namibia was a wealthy diamond town, until the sand came and the miners had to leave.

The plants succeeded in holding the sand in place, but as a result no sand could drift inland to rebuild the dunes in their original location. Those inland dunes have still not recovered.

Too Many Wheels

Dune areas all over the United States are used in many ways, for walking and observing animals, but also for off-road vehicles. Dune buggies and motorcycles leave scars that last for a long time—they can crush sensitive plants and collapse animal **burrows.**

Sand pressed down by tires is harder for the wind to move, and this can stop the natural process of dune building. By disturbing vegetation, off-road vehicles can also speed up **erosion** and make dunes drift faster than normal.

Guess What?

Wheel tracks made by the diamond miners of Kolmanskop in the Namib Desert are still clearly visible nearly a hundred years after they were made.

Dunes on the shore of Lake Ontario were cleared of trees in around 1783. In the next eight years the dunes moved 150 ft (45 m) and sand was blown inland for 2 mi (3 km).

Imperial Sand Dunes in California is an area where people use off-road vehicles. They are fun for people, but bad for the dunes.

Faraway Dunes

All over the world, as well as in the United States, dunes are threatened. Visitors flock to the most famous areas, like the dunes on the coast of Namibia, but people's actions threaten to spoil the beauty they have come to see. Near the roads that go through the dunes, the landscape is littered with the remains of fires and garbage left by campers.

Trash left behind by people spoils the beauty of the sand dunes and can also be harmful to the animals that live there.

Tough Survivors

But dunes are tough. The forces that built them, **erosion** and wind, are still active today. Although visitors might damage their beauty, the dunes will recover in time—if they are left to themselves.

Beauty for Tomorrow

The animals and plants of the dune **microhabitat** have taken millions of years to **evolve** their delicate balance. We should be careful not to disturb them. Humans threaten sand dunes mostly by driving vehicles over them.

Harsh but beautiful, the dunes of Death Valley National Park in California are a treasure worth protecting for generations to come.

If we walk or ride animals there instead, and are careful of plants and **burrows,** we can enjoy the beauty of the dunes and leave them unharmed so that future generations can also enjoy them.

Guess What?

Peirson's milkvetch is a plant that grows on California's Algodones Dunes. It has been saved from near extinction by a ban of off-road vehicles from over half the dune area.

A sport called sandboarding is posing a threat to some sand dunes. Sandboarders "surf" down dunes on boards, often damaging plants and disturbing animals.

Glossary

abdomen rear of an insect's body, behind the head and thorax

adapted changed; over time animals frequently adapt or change to suit their environments

amphibian animal that can live in water and on land

bask lie in the sun

burrow dig a hole or the hole itself

condense turn from vapor into liquid, like steam into water

downwind facing away from the direction in which the wind is blowing

erode wear away

erosion process of wearing away

evolve change gradually over many generations

forage search for food

invertebrate animal that does not have a backbone

larva first stage of an insect's life, after it hatches from the egg

litter young born to the same animal at the same time

microhabitat a small specialized environment, such as a sand dune, where particular animals live and plants grow

paralyze make a creature unable to move

pioneer the first person, plant, or animal to live somewhere

predator animal or plant that kills animals to eat

prey food of a predator

slip face sloping side of a dune away from the direction of the wind, where the sand grains slip down

specialist one who has become very good at solving a particular kind of problem. An animal is a specialist if it has developed special ways of surviving in a specific environment.

venomous producing poison

water vapor water in gas form

windward facing toward the direction from which the wind is blowing

Further Reading

Allaby, Michael and Robert Anderson. *Biomes Atlases: Deserts and Semideserts.* Chicago: Raintree, 2003.

Peterson, David. *Great Sand Dunes National Monument.* Danbury, Conn.: Scholastic Library, 2000.

Rager, Ellen J. and Nancy Woodman (illus). *Sand.* Washington D.C.: National Geographic Society, 2000.

Index

Algodones Dunes, California 29
ant lion 15
ants 4, 15, 16, 17, 19
    ant nests 17
aphids 17

beach grass (see marram grass)
beetles 14
    darkling beetles 14
    tiger beetle 5, 15
birds of prey 24
    hawks 24
    owls 24
burrows 8, 12, 13, 15, 16, 23, 27, 29

crickets 16

Death Valley National Park 29
digger wasps (see sand wasps)
drifting dunes 26, 27
dune buggies (see off-road vehicles)
dune building 6, 7
dune plants 10, 11, 15, 16, 26, 29
    sand verbena 4, 11
    sea rocket 5, 11
    seaside spurge 4, 11
    tumbleweed 11

elephants 25
erosion 6, 27, 28

gerbil 8
Gran Desierto (see Sonoran Desert)
grasshoppers 16, 17

desert locust 17
Great Sand Dunes National Monument, Colorado 5

honeydew 17

Imperial Sand Dunes, California 27

kangaroo rat (see rodents)

Lake Ontario 27
lions 25
litter 28
lizards 8, 9, 13, 18–19,
    basking 18, 19
    horned lizard 18, *19*
    legless lizard 4
    sand-diving 9

marram grass 10, 26
motorcycles (see off-road vehicles)

Namib Desert 11, 13, 14, 25, 28
    Kolmanskop 26, 27
nara bush 11
natterjack toad 25

off-road vehicles 27, 28, 29
Oregon coastal dunes 26

Peirson's milkvetch 29
people and dunes 25, 26, 27, 28, 29
"pioneer plants" (see dune plants)
plant bugs (see aphids)

plants (see dune plants)

rodents 22–23
    kangaroo mouse 23
    kangaroo rats 5, 22, 23, 24

sand grain formation 6, 7
sand wasps 5, 12, 13, 15
sandboarding 29
"singing dunes" 9
slip face 7, 8, 9
snakes 20–21
    black mamba 21
    fer de lance 20
    heat-sensitive pits 21
    rattlesnakes 4, 20, 21, 23
    sidewinder 20, 21
    tongues 21
Sonoran Desert 5
specialists 5, 11, 24
spiders 13, 15
    cartwheel spider 13
    trapdoor spider 4, 13

threats to dunes 26–27

water vapor 11
wind 4, 6, 7, 9, 28